CHILDREN'S BOOKS FROM THE PAST

VOLUME 1

IMAGES OF THE OLD TESTAMENT

CHILDREN'S BOOKS FROM THE PAST

A Series of Reprints Reproduced
in Facsimile from the Osborne Collection
of Early Children's Books
(1505-1910)

In Co-operation
with the Toronto Public Library

Volume 1

Images of the
Old Testament

Hans Holbein, the Younger

PREFACE BY
MARGARET MALONEY

HERBERT LANG
BERN AND FRANKFURT/M.
1973

ISBN 3 261 01003 7
Herbert Lang & Co, Ltd., Publishers, Bern and Frankfurt/M.
© Toronto Public Library, Toronto (Canada), 1973

Printed by Reda S.A. Chêne-Bourg, Geneva
Switzerland

Preface to The Images of the Old Testament

The Images of the Old Testament was first published in 1538 with Latin title and descriptive text. While this edition bore the device of the printers, Melchior and Gaspar Trechsel, and the publishers' imprint address (Under the Shield of Cologne at Lyons) of the Frellon brothers, Jean (Johan) and François, it failed, surprisingly, to identify the artist, Hans Holbein.

Holbein was born of an artistic family in Augsburg, Swabia, in 1497 and died of plague in London, Michaelmas, 1543. About 1515 he moved to Basle, Switzerland, drawn by the freedom and stimulation of the humanist revival revolving around Erasmus. Basle was also a principal centre of the book trade under the prominent printer, Johann Froben.

By the early 1520's the Reformation was at high tide. Reading and dissemination of Scripture in the vernacular was spurred by the publication, at Wittenberg in 1522, of Luther's German translation of the New Testament, accompanied by woodcuts to amplify preaching to the unlettered and the young. Amid such a receptive climate Holbein probably began designing his Old Testament cuts, drawing in pen and ink directly on wood. The actual engraving was done by a "stamp cutter", most likely the expert craftsman, Hans Lützelburger (1495?-1526), a known associate. However, after Lützelburger's death the blocks passed into other hands, perhaps to the printing firm of the Trechsels who may have originally commissioned the series. The discrepancy in quality of a few cuts admits the possibility of completion by an inferior engraver or even of the addition of designs other than Holbein's. The religious upheaval of the times delayed their publication for over a decade. Indeed circumstances were so altered by 1526 that Erasmus recorded that "the arts are stagnating" at Basle and furnished Holbein with an introductory letter to Sir Thomas More at the court of Henry VIII. After two years abroad Holbein returned briefly to Basle but found that Erasmus had left, that Froben was dead, and that the Iconoclasts, in the wake of Zwingli, had zealously plundered and destroyed much religious art. By the spring of 1532 he retreated permanently to England.

The English court was also in crisis. More had resigned as Lord Chancellor, Wolsey had fallen. Henry was negotiating an anulment from Catherine of Aragon to allow his marriage to Anne Boleyn. Holbein avoided his former circles and moved instead in the company of his countrymen, the merchant goldsmiths of the Hanseatic League at the Steelyard.

Following Henry's break with Rome, Holbein returned to court. Among his commissions were woodcuts for the title-pages of the Coverdale Bible (1535) and the Cranmer or Great Bible (1539). By 1536 Holbein was designated "the king's painter". He decorated the Privy Chamber Wall at Whitehall and painted Anne Boleyn, Jane Seymour, Anne of Cleves and Catherine Howard.

Holbein's fame at Henry VIII's court must have been an incentive in the initial publication of his long neglected *Images of the Old Testament* and also provided a justification for the 1549 edition with English and French text. It was also in England in 1535 that the artist met and did a portrait of Nicolas Bourbon of Vandoeuvre (1503-1550), a French poet-scholar, employed as court tutor to Anne Boleyn's nephew. This same Bourbon, resident in Lyons by 1539, composed for the second edition of the *Images*, an address, in Latin distichs with a Greek epigram, identifying the designer of the ninety-four unsigned woodcuts as Hans Holbein, the younger. In true Renaissance style the poet compared his friend to the masters of antiquity, lauding him as the Apelles of his age.

The immediate and prolonged success of the *Images* led to many editions between 1538 and 1549, with frequent changes, errors and different language combinations. (These are clarified in the excellent catalogue of French sixteenth century books compiled by Ruth Mortimer of Harvard University Library). Among these variations the bibliographer Brunet terms this unique English and French edition, here reproduced in facsimile, "plus rare que les autres".

François Frellon's editorial preface, included since the first edition, urged readers to spurn the seductive images of such goddesses as Venus and Diana, celebrated in fable and poetry, and to turn instead to the visual contemplation of Holy Scripture.

Gilles Corrozet (1510-1568), a humanist poet, contributed a French verse preface (first appearing in the 1539 edition), which forms a rhyming paraphrase of Frellon's. He also wrote the French quatrains which parallel the English text (a literal translation of the earlier descriptive Latin). The poet's motto was "Plus que moins".

In light of Corrozet's preface which refers to the *Images of the Old Testament* as so designed that large and small, young and old will have pleasure of heart and eye –

Et si faictes ainsi,
Grandz & petis, les ieunes & les vieulx
Auront plaisir, & au cœur & aux yeulx —

this work must be considered one of the earliest picture books combining pleasure and instruction for children, particularly within the context of its time, when scripture reading dominated the education of youth. It predated by forty-two years Jost Amman's *Kunst- und Lehrbüchlein* published in 1580 at Zurich.

Three hundred years later, in 1843, eight of Holbein's Old Testament designs were re-engraved on wood and used to illustrate *Bible Events*, one of the earliest titles in the famous Home Treasury series edited by Felix Summerly (Sir Henry Cole).

The Frellon name and device permanently replaced those of the Trechsel brothers after 1543 on the title page of the *Images*. Their crab and butterfly with the word "matura" combined to symbolize that "hastening slowly produces mature works". The ornamental initials, one with *putti* (cherubs) and one foliated with a bird, were probably from the publisher's stock. The four medallion cuts of the Evangelists (on the verso of leaf N3), by another artist, were appended first to the 1547 edition.

The Frellons and the Trechsels, like many Lyons publishers and printers, had ties in Basle. Holbein himself undoubtedly visited Lyons, which was a thriving commercial and cosmopolitan city actively engaged in trade with Germany and Switzerland. After the death of François in 1546 Jean Frellon continued the business alone until 1568, and despite his overt protestant sympathies took an active part in the municipal affairs of staunchly Catholic Lyons.

The first four and smaller woodcuts of the *Images* were taken from the beginning of Holbein's *Dance of Death*, also printed by M. and G. Trechsel for J. and F. Frellon at Lyons in 1538. This famous series was contemporary in design with the *Images*, with one block monogrammed by the engraver, Hans Lützelburger, but similarly delayed in publication. Holbein's Old Testament cuts were used subsequently in various folio Bibles issued at Lyons and may have been initially planned for this purpose rather than the small quarto edition which first appeared.

The copy held by the Osborne Collection bears irregularities. For Exodus III and V, cuts and text have been transposed, as have the Paralipomenon (Chronicles) blocks of the musicians and Solomon at the altar. The binding is contemporary and possibly the original vellum.

Margaret Maloney
Toronto Public Library

THE
IMAGES
OF THE OLD
TESTAMENT,

Lately expreſſed, ſet forthe in Yngliſhe and
Frenche, vuith a playn and
brief expoſition.

MATVRA.

Printid at Lyons, by Iohan Frellon, the
yere of our lord God, 1 5 4 9.

Franciscus Frellonius Christiano Lectori, S.

En tibi, Christiane lector, sacrorum canonum tabulas, cum earundem & Latina & Gallica interpretatione officiose exhibemus: Illud in primis admonentes, vt reiectis Veneris, & Dianæ, cæterarúmque dearũ libidinosis imaginibus, quæ animum vel errore impediunt, vel turpitudine labefactãt, ad has sacrosanctas Iconas, quæ Hagiographorum penetralia digito commonstrant, omnes tui conatus referantur. Quid enim pulchrius, aut Christiano homine dignius, quàm ad has res animũ adiicere, quæ solæ fidei mysteria sapiunt, & Deum creatorem nostrum vnicè amare, ac veram religionem profiteri præcipiũt? Tuum igitur erit hunc nostrum laborem æquo animo suscipere, ac cæteros commonefacere, vt eiusmodi omnia ad Dei largitoris beneficentissimi gloriam, & honorem dirigere meminerint. Vale Lector, & fruere.

Nicolai Borbonii Vando-

perani Poetæ Lingonensis

Ad Lectorem Carmen.

VPER in Elysio cùm fortè erra-
   ret Apelles,
   Vna aderat Zeusis, Parrhasiúsque
   comes.
Hi duo multa satis fundebant verba:sed ille
   Intereà mœrens & taciturnus erat.
Mirantur comites, faríque hortâtur,& vrgét:
   Suspirans imo pectore Coûs,ait:
O famæ ignari,superis quæ nuper ab oris
   (Vana vt inã)Stygias venit ad vsq; domos:
Scilicet,esse hodie quendã ex mortalibus vnũ,
   Ostendat qui me vósque fuisse nihil:
Qui nos declaret Pictores nomine tantúm,
   Picturæque omneis antè fuisse rudes.
Holbius est homini nomé,qui nomina nostra
   Obscura ex claris,ac propè nulla facit.
Talis apud Manes querimonia fertur:& illos
   Sic equidem meritò censeo posse queri.

Nã tabulã ſi quis videat,quã pinxerit Hanſus
   Holbius,ille artis gloria prima ſuæ:
Protinus exclamet,Potuit Deus edere mõſtrũ
   Quod video:humanæ nõ potuêre manus.
Icones hæ ſacræ tanti ſunt (optime lector)
   Artificis, dignum quod venerêris opus.
Proderit hac pictura animum pauiſſe ſalubri,
   Quæ tibi diuinas exprimit hiſtorias.
Tradidit arcano quæcũque volumine Moſes,
   Tótque alii vates,gens agitata Deo,
His H A N S I tabulis repræſentantur: & vnà
   Interpres rerum ſermo Latinus adeſt.
Hæc legito:Valeat rapti Ganymedis amator:
   Síntque procul Cypriæ turpia furta Deæ.

Eiuſdem Borbonij Poetæ.

Δίςιχον.
Ωξέρ' ἰδὴρ ἔιδωλα θέλᾳς ἐμπνοῖσιρ ὁμοῖα,
   Ολβἴακῆς ἔγγιεο δέγκεο τᐤτο χερός.

Latinè idem penè ad verbum.

Cernere vis,hoſpes,ſimulacra ſimillima viuis?
Hoc opus Holbinæ nobile cerne manus.

Gilles Corrozet

Aux Lecteurs.

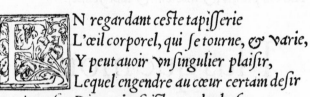

N regardant ceste tapisserie
L'œil corporel, qui se tourne, & varie,
Y peut auoir vn singulier plaisir,
Lequel engendre au cœur certain desir
D'aimer son Dieu, qui a faict tant de choses
Dedans la letre, & saincte Bible encloses.

Ces beaux portraictz seruiront d'exemplaire,
Monstrant qu'il fault au Seigneur Dieu complaire:
Exciteront de luy faire seruice,
Retireront de tout peché & vice:
Quand ilz seront insculpez en l'esprit,
Comme ilz sont painctz, & couchez par escrit.

Donques ostez de voz maisons, & salles
Tant de tapis, & de painctures salles,
Ostez Venus, & son filz Cupido,
Ostez Heleine, & Phyllis, & Dido,

Ostez du tout fables & poesies,
Et receuez meilleures fantasies.

    Mettez au lieu, & soyent voz chambres ceinctes
Des dictz sacréz, & des histoires sainctes,
Telles que sont celles que voyez cy
En ce liuret. Et si faictes ainsi,
Grandz & petis, les ieunes & les vieulx
Auront plaisir, & au cœur & aux yeulx,

Plus que moins.

By the vuord of almygthy god ar created
and blyſſed the erthe, day nygte, heuen,
the ſey, the ſon, mon, ſters, fyches, and
beyſts of the erth. Adam and Heua ar alſo created.

GENESIS I.

Dieu fit le ciel dés le commencement,
Puis terre, & mer, & tout humain ouurage:
Adam, & Heue il fit femblablement
Pleins de raiſon forméz à ſon image.

Adam is ſet in paradiſo of pleaſure to vuhon
ys forbedden the tre of life. The ſuttelty
off the ſerpent Adã, and Heua ar deceaued.

GENESIS   II. & III.

Dieu leur deffend que de l'arbre de vie
Ne mangent fruict, ſur peine de la Mort:
Mais le ſerpent, ayant ſur eux enuie,
Fait tant qu'Adam au fruict de l'arbre mord.

Vuhen Adam and Heua dyd atknolege thor
syn, they dyd fle from the face of God, and
ar obiected vnto deth. Cherubim is feth lefo
re paradife of pleafur vuyth a fyrey fvuord.

GENESIS III.

Pour le peché qu'ilz feirent contre Dieu,
Furent maudictz chacun felon l'offence:
Puis Cherubim les met hors de cé lieu,
Et contre mort n'eurent plus de defence.

B

Adam expelled ouut off Paradyſe is cóman-
ded to dyge and plouu the erth, the vuomã
ys ſubiect vnto the man, and bringeth forht
hyr chylder in ſorouue.

GENESIS   III.

En grand labeur, & ſueur de ſon corps
Le pere Adam a ſa vie gaignée,
Heue tandis en doloreux effortz,
Subiecte à l'Homme enfante ſa lignée.

Rygthus Noe by the cōmandement of God
goyth in to the shyppe he and his ar saued
al, other deſtroed, The rauen and the doue
letten ouut of the ſyppe.

GENESIS   VII.

Tous les humains par l'uniuers deluge
Furent peris: Noé le Patriarche
Par le vouloir de Dieu, & pour refuge,
Auec les ſiens, entra dedans ſon arche.

The touure of Babylon is bylded, vuherupon
cometh confusion of languages.

GENESIS.   XI.

Nembroth geant commença à construire
La tour Babel, dicte confusion:
Mais Dieu voulant si grand orgueil destruire,
Es langues mist toute diuision.

Abraham logieh the Angels, Iſaac is promyſed vnto hym, Sara lauugot behynd the dore
of the tabernacle. The deſtruction of the So-
domites is ſheuued vnto Abraham. Abraham
prayth for the Sodomiths.

GENESIS   XVIII.

A Abraham les Anges ont promis,
D'auoir vn filz, Sara n'en fait que rire:
A deux genoux pour Sodome ſ'eſt mis,
En priant Dieu de retarder ſon ire.

B   3

The fayth of Abraham is tented He is commanded to offer hys son Isaac. The Angel doth cal vnto Abraham, thar he shuld not kylle hys son.

GENESIS   XXII.

Dieu commanda à Abraham de faire,
De son enfant Isaac sacrifice:
Au mandement voulant doncq' satisfaire,
Dieu fut content de sa foy & iustice.

Iacob by the ſutteltye of his mother takyth the blyſſing from Eſau. Iſaac is ſoro fulle. Eſau is conforted.

Le bon Iacob par conſeil de ſa mere,
Eut d'Iſaac la benediction:
En ſe faignant eſtre Eſau ſon frere,
Qui ſe marrit de la deception.

B 4

Ioſeph by cauſe he accuſed his brether and
had dremed, is caſten in the cyſtern, he dely
ucred ouut of the cyſtern, is ſolde vnto the
Iſmaelyts.

GENESIS   XXXVII.

L'enfant Ioſeph fut mis en la ciſterne,
Pour vn ſien ſonge à ſes freres predict,
Mais du Seigneur la prouidence eterne
A des marchans permiſt qu'on le vendit.

Pharaos dreme of the seuen oxen and ears of
corn, Ioseph delyuered ouut of pryson doth
expouund it, tte is maed reuuber ouer Egypte.

Au souef dormir Pharaon se dispose,
Sept espicz voit, & sept beufz en songeant,
Ioseph mis hors de prison, luy expose:
Qui sur Egypte est faict maistre, & regent.

Vuhen Iacob shuld dye, he porcheſſyth vnto him Ephraim and Manaſſes the ſons of Io
ſeph: and blyſſyth them.

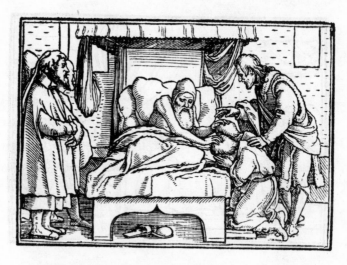

Iacob voyant le ſien eage prefix,
Et qu'il eſtoit bien pres deſ ſr. deces,
Il adopta de Ioſeph les deux filx,
L'un Ephraim, & l'autre Manaſſes.

Ioſeph is buryed. The chylder of Iſrael ar op
preſſed in Egypte vuyth hard bódage, The
diligence of grod meduuyues ys expreſſed.

EXODI.   I.

Ioſeph eſt mort, & mis en ſepulture,
Iſrael ſouffre vne grand tyrannie,
Matrones ſont de ſi doulce nature,
Qu'elles ont ſauué à tous maſles la vie.

Moyſes and Aaron goyth vnto Pharao, The
peple ar mor and mor oppreſſed . Moyſes
and Aaron ar accuſed of the peple.

E X O D I   V.

Auec ſon frere eſt Moyſe adreſſé
Vers Pharaon, priant pour Iſrael:
De plus en plus fut le peuple oppreſſé
Par celuy Roy, & ſon peuple cruel.

Moyſes fedyth the sheyp. He ſeyth God in
the buſhe, He is ſent vnto the chylder of Iſrahel, and vnto Pharao the oppreſſed.

E X O D I   III.

Le bon Moyſe en ſes brebis gardant,
Fut enuoyé au peuple Iſraelite
De Dieu, qu'il vit en vn buiſſon ardant,
Auſſy deuers Pharaon roy d'Egypte.

Pharaos hart ys hardenyt, he doth perseuu
the Israhelites and is drouudet. The Israheli
tes grugith, desparyng of ther helth. They
go thorouu the myds of the sey vuyth dry
fete, vuhen they had gotten the victori they
vuor shipped God.

F X O D I   XIIII & XV.

Tous les enfans d'Israel s'amasserent,
La rouge mer leur feit voye, au deuant
Partit ses eaux, tant qu'a pied sec passerent:
Mais Pharaon fut noyé les suyuant.

The Ifrahelits goyth forth in to the vuylker-
nes of Sin, vuen they mormured for mete,
God ranyth them quuales and manna.

EXODI   XVI.

Iceux paſſés, ilz ſe mettent en voye
Dens les deſertz: & pour mieulx les pourueoir,
Noſtre Seigneur la manne leur enuoye,
Qu'il leur faiſoit du ciel en bas plouuoir.

The Iſærelites doyth lay ther tents at the
mount of Synay. The people is cõmanded
to do ſacrifice. Almighty God appeoyth
vuyth lighning and thoundaryng, that the
people ſhud feare hym.

EXODI   XIX.

Ceulx d'Iſrael eſtablirent leurs tentes
En Sinai, chaſcun ſe ſanctifie:
Puis par tonnerre, & par fouldres patentes
Noſtre Seigneur ſa grandeur notifie.

The Iſrahelits ar cōmanded to make an Ark,
a table, and a kandelſtyke for the offerryng
of fyrſt fruts vnto God. The shea breds ar
ſet vpon the table.

E X O D I   XXV.

L'arche ſe faict,la belle table,auſſi
Le chandelier,par diſpoſition
De noſtre Dieu,ſur ceſte table cy
On met les pains de propoſition.

D

Vuhen Moyſes had reſtored the tables, he
vuent into the hille, he deſireth God to go
vuith the peple. The company of Gentiles,
and idolatry is forbydden.

E X O D I   XXXIIII.

Dieu eſcriuit les Tables de la loy,
Moyſe enclin à deux genoux, le prie
Pour Iſrael, en ferme, & viue foy:
Dieu luy defend payenne idolatrie.

Moyſes is inſtructed of the lord ouut of the
tabernacle of vuyttnes, houu he ſhal offer
oxen and ſhepe.

LEVITICI I.

Dieu à Moyſe enſeigna ſon office,
Luy demonſtrant par mandementz nouueaux,
Comme il conuient faire le ſacrifice
Des gras moutons, des vaches, & des veaux.

D 2

Moyſes by the cōmandement of the lord, al
the peple gathered befor the dores of the ta
bernacle, conſecratyth Aaron and bys chyl
der.

LEVITICI   VIII.

Au mandement de Dieu le createur,
Preſent le peuple, Aaron fut ſacré
Sur Iſrael, grand Eueſque & paſteur,
Et tous ſes filz chaſcun en ſon degré.

Nadab and Abiu, the sons of Aaron, contrary
to Gods commandement offeryng strange
fyre, ar consumed vuyth the flamme.

LEVITICI X.

Nadab, auec Abiu, pour autant
Que feu estrange au Seigneur Dieu offrirent,
Contre son vueil (leur orgueil abatant)
Par feu soudain entre flammes perirent.

D 3

The lord sheuuyth the commandements vnto Moyſes , ſum Moral, and ſum Ceremo-
nial.

LEVITICI XIX.

Deſſus le mont Dieu enſeigne à Moyſe
Ses mandementz, qui ſont les Loix Morales:
Puis luy apprent l'obſeruance,& la guiſe,
Pour accomplir les Ceremoniales.

Moyſes and Aaron doth numbre men that
vuen abbe to fygth acorrdyng vnto the tu-
uelue tribes of Iſrahel. The Tribe of Leui is
ordined for the tabernacle.

Moyſe eſlit, & nombre entierement
Les hommes fortz, de vaillance ennoblis,
Ceux de Leui ont le gouuernement
Du tabernacle, ou ilz ſont eſtablis.

Moyſes and Aaron, the princes of famylies,
aaer dyng vnto Gods commandement re-
herſed, doth orden ſtations of the tents.

NVMERI   II.

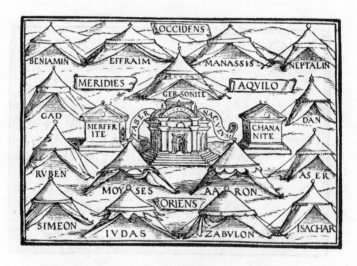

Apres moyſe (au mandement de Dieu)
A ceux qui ſont des familles les princes,
Il ordonna leur aſſiete & leur lieu,
En trauerſant les pays, & prouinces.

Core, Dathan and Abiron grudgyng agaiuſt
Moyſes , ar ſuualo vued vp of the erth
vuyth many othor.

Core, Dathan, & Abiron murmurent,
Contre Moyſe & ſon authorité:
Mais tout ſubit en terre abſorbez furent.
Comme chaſcun auoit bien merité.

E

Ifrahel rebellyng ys plaged vuith fyry Serpens. Moyfes doth feth vp a Brafen Serpent,
for a token: the vuhyche vuhen they that
vuar bitten dyd behold, they vuar hole.

NVMERI   XXI.

Par les Serpens ardens l'homme greué,
Pour y trouuer remede fouuerain,
Eſtoit guery, quand il auoit leué
Le ſien regard vers le Serpent d'ærain.

The Iſrahelits vuhen they had ouercóne the
Madianits, they brogth the pray vnto Moy
ſes and Aaron. they dyd reſerue the virgi-
nis, the vuhomé ar killed. The pra iis equal-
lye deuided.

NVMERI   XXXI.

Du tout deſſaictz ſont les Madianites
(La vierge ſauue) eſt toute femme occiſe,
Par les vainqueurs hommes Iſraelites:
Et puis entre eux la proye ſe diuiſe.

Moyſes in the vuyldernes repetyth the thyn
ge vuhych vuar done in the hille Horeb,he
doth conſtitute the Princes off the pople
vuyth hym.

Moyſe compte, & à entendre donne
Ce qui fut faiƈt,depuis le partement
Du mont Horeb.Puis auec ſoy ordonne
Des Gouuerneurs,pour ſon ſupportement.

Moyſes not only openly but alſo sharply
monyſheth the peple of berning and folou-
uyng the commandements of God.

Moyſe apres aigrement admoneſte,
Ceux d'Iſrael d'apprendre & obſeruer
La Loy de Dieu bonne, ſaincte & honeſte,
Et ſes preceptz (tant bien faiſtz) conſeruer.

Moyses iudgeth diligontly of the lyuing of Preſts and Leuites. Chriſt is promyſed. That a fals prophet shuld be kylled, and houu he shalbe knouuyn.

Moyſe à ſoing du viure des Leuites,
Et Ieſus Chriſt eſt aux hommes promis.
Le faulx prophete à ſes mœurs hypocrites
Eſt recongneu. & doit eſtre à mort mis.

Iosue vuyth the host of Israhelites doth kyl
the rings be yond Iordane.

IOSVE   XII.

Iosué Duc d'Israel quand il eut
Passé Iordain auec son exercite,
Trente & vn Roy il occit, puis esleut
La terre aux siens, & chascun lieu limite.

Iudas the Captaine of the Israhelites ouercō-
myth the Chananyse. Adonibezec, his hend
and his fete cur of, is bedde pryfoner in to
Ierufalem.

Le Duc Iudas Chananée guerroye,
Et pris captif Adonibezec Roy,
Les piedz, & mains luy tranche, & puis l'enuoye
A la cité, en fi piteux arroy.

Ruth glenyng ears of corn in Booz felde,
fand fauor before hym, the ears vuhyche
she had gathered beryth she vnto hyr mother in lauu.

R V T H   II.

Ruth va aux champs pour le bled, qui restoit
Aux moissonneurs, en espicz recueillir,
Deuant Booz (à qui le champ estoit)
Grace trouua, qui la feit accueillir.

F

Anna the vuyfe of Elcane beyng long ba-
rand, doth obtaine of God hyr fon Samuel,
by caufe she praed from hyr hareth, Heli
the Preft fittyng in a chare befor the dores
of the temple of God.

I. REGVM I.

Anne ne peut d'Elcana fon mary
Auoir enfans, mais le Seigneur receut
Son oraifon faicte de cœur marry,
Et luy donna que Samuel conceut.

Saul is annoynted of Samuel kyng ouer Iſrahel. a token is gyuen him ath the graue of
Rachel, vuherby he shuld knoa that he vuas annoynted kyng of God.

Par Samuel prophete ſainct, & digne
Saul eſt oinct Roy deſſus Iſrael:
Et pour le croire il luy donne le ſigne
De ſeureté pres le tumbeau Rachel.

Dauid castyng auuay Saul harnes, and tri-
sting only in the pouur of God, vuyth a
stone ouut of hys styng kyllyth Goliath he
chasyth auuay the Philistians.

I.   REGVM   XVII.

Dauid occit Goliath d'une pierre,
Sans estre armé, en Dieu se confiant.
Par vn enfant le geant mis par terre,
Des Philistins l'ost retourne fuyant.

It is sheuued Dauid that Ceilam vuas by se-
ged of the Philistians. He takyng consel of
the lord, deliuerid Ceilã from the Philistiãs.

On a noncé au preux Dauid, comment
Des Philistins Ceile est assaillie:
Ayant de Dieu prins conseil doublement,
La deliura faisant sur eux saillie.

F 3

The deth of Saul and Ionathan is sheuued vn
to Dauid. He is sorouuful, and commandith
hym to be kylled vuhyche fained hym self
to haue kylled Saul.

II.   Regvm   I.

Vng faux herault au Roy Dauid reuele,
Le Roy Saul & son filz estre mort,
Pensant porter quelque bonne nouuelle:
Mais pour le faict vanté, fut mis à mort.

Dauid chaſeth auuay the Philiſtians, and ma
keth them tributary vnto hym. Adarezer
kyng Soba is ſmytten.

II.   Regvm   VIII.

Le Roy Dauid fait à ſoy tributaires
Les Philiſtins, anciens ennemis,
Et en fin vient à chef de ſes contraires,
Adarezer Roy de Sobe à mort mis.

F 4

Dauid callith Vriam from the hoſt, by cauſe
he vuold the adultery vuych he had com-
mitted vuyth hys vuyſe, shud be hylde.
Vrias vuhen he had receu id letters of Dauid, retornyth vnto the hoſt, and ther is he
kylled.

Dauid voulant l'adultere celer,
Mande Vrias, & luy baille vne lettre:
Puis luy commande à la bataille aller,
Par telle fraude il le feit à mort mettre.

Nathan the Prophet accuſytd Dauid of mur
der ſheuuyng hym a parable of the ryche
man and the puor. Rabbath a cyty of the
Ammonits is ouercomne of Dauid.

Nathan adreſſe à Dauid ſa parole
Pour l'homicide ayant eſté commis,
Et le reprint par vne parabole:
Deuant Rabbath auſſy le ſiege eſt mis.

G

Abſalon by the ſuttelty and vuyſdŏ of Ioab,
and the vuhoman of Thecuid, is called aga-
ine, Dauid doth kyſſe hys ſon Abſalon.

II.   Regvm   XIIII.

Par le moyen d'une femme, & prudence,
Tant fait Ioab, que Dauid ſe rapaiſe
Vers Abſalom, qui vient en reuerence
S'humilier, & ſon pere le baiſe.

Amaſa callyth to gyther Iudam againſt Se-
bam:vuhom Ioab kyſſed,and in ther iornay
at the great ſton deſat fully kylled.

II.   Regvm   XX.

Amaſa vient d'aſſembler gens de guerre
Contre Seba,& Ioab le ſalue
Par trahiſon aupres de la grand pierre,
Et en faignant de l'embraſſer,le tue.

G 2

Abiſag the fare maden is gyuen vnto old Da
uid vuhyche ſhuld kepe hym vuarm vuhen
he ſlepyth.

III.   R E G V M   I.

Quand Dauid fut deuenu foible & vieux,
On luy bailla Abiſag la pucelle,
Pour l'eſchauffer, qui ſans faict vicieux.
Par maintes nuictz dormit auec icelle.

Hiram ſcudith hys ſeruants that he mygth re
ioie vuyth Salomon.   Salomon requirith
tymbrt of Hiram for the bueldyng of the
temple.

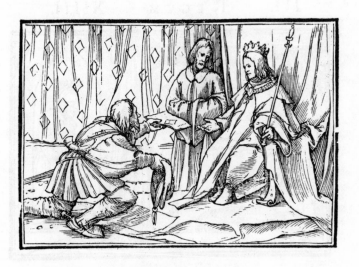

Le roy Hiram ſes ſeruiteurs enuoye
Vers Salomon, auec ſalut treſample:
Lors le requiert Salomon qu'il pouruoye
Luy donner bois pour conſtruire ſon temple.

Ieroboam confultyth Ahiam the prophet, by
hys vuyfe, as côcerning the helth of his fon
vuhyche vuas feyk. but as fon as fhe vuas
comne hom and entered in ath the dore,
Abia dyed.

III. R E G V M XIIII.

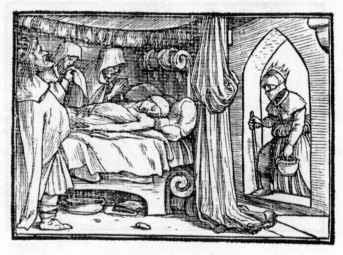

Ieroboam enuoye fon efpoufe,
Pour de fon filz malade f'enquerir
Vers Abias, qui fa mort luy propofe,
Et elle entraut l'enfant f'en va mourir.

Elias sheuuyth vnto the preyſts of Baal, that
God of Iſrahel vuas the very true God, God
teſtifiyng the ſame by the fyre conſumyng
the offeryng of Elias. The preyſts of Baal
ar kylled.

Elie met le beuf deſſus l'autel,
Le feu du ciel deſcend ſans artifice,
Et pour monſtrer que le Dieu d'Iſrael
Eſt le vray Dieu, bruſle le ſacrifice.

G 4

Elias deuidit the vuater vuith his kloke. He
receued vp in to heuem can not be fouund.
The bays vuhiche dyd mok Elyseus ar rẽt
druouured of the Bears.

IIII.　　Regvm　　II.

Cheuaux ardens rauirent, & leuerent
Elie en l'air, dedans vn char de feu:
Deux ours du bois les enfans estranglerent,
Lesquelz auoyent moqué l'homme de Dieu.

Ioiada the Byshope, Athalia beyng kylled,
maketh Ioas kyng ouer Iſrahel, Mathan the
preſt of Baal is kylled befor the altare.

IIII.   REGVM   XI.

Par Ioiada, Ioas conſtitué
Sur Iſrael fut en l'eſtat Royal:
Et Mathan preſbtre idolatre tué,
Deuant l'autel de ſon faulx Dieu Baal.

H

Achaz kyng of Iuda ful of idolatry, doth cõ
fecrat hys fon by the fire. Ierufalem is byfe-
ged and requireth hely of the kyng of the
Affyrians.

IIII.   R E G V M   X V I.

Le Roy Achaz idolatre deuint,
En feu ardant son filz il sacrifie:
Puis quand la guerre encontre luy suruint,
Secours demande au Roy d'Aßyrie.

Iosias redith the boke of Deuteronomy before the peple, He destroyth Idols, and kyllyth the preysts of Baal.

IIII.   REGVM.   XXIII.

Le Roy Iosie au peuple Iudaique,
Deuteronome il lit de bout en bout:
Et son pays purgeant d'erreur inique,
Il fait brusler les idoles par tout.

I. PARALIP. I.

Icy recite & nombre briefuement
Iusqu'a Iacob, la genealogie,
Depuis Adam, dés le commencement,
Qui fut soubz Dieu gouuernée & regie.

Saul fygthyng vnlukkyly aganſt the Philiſtians, kyllyth hym ſelf. his harnes is conſe-
crat in the temple of his God. buth his hed
is caryed of the Philiſtians in to the temple
of idoles.

Saul faiſant la guerre aux Philiſtins,
Soy meſme occit, quand ſa perte contemple:
Les Philiſtins entre tous leurs butins,
Portent le chef de Saul en leur temple.

H 3

Dauid vuhen the ark vuas brogth, agayn
blyſſyth the peple, and makyth then alſo a
feſt. He doth inſtruit the miniſters of the
ark to prayſe God in inſtrumēts of muſyke.

I. PARALIP. XVI.

Le Roy Dauid deuant l'Arche de Dieu.
Benit le peuple, & à manger luy donne:
Et pour louer le Seigneur, au ſainct lieu
Muſiciens, & inſtrumens ordonne.

Salomon grith in to the hye place Gabaon
to do ſacrifice, he requirith of God yuiſdō,
and knologe to iudge the peple.

En Gabaon Salomon ſacrifie,
Puis prie à Dieu luy donner ſageſſe:
Dieu parle à luy, & ſi luy certifie
Qu'il luy donra Sapience, & Richeſſe.

Salomon prayth for the congregation. He
thankyth God, vuhyche fulfyld the promy
ſes mad vnto Dauid. He deſyrith of God
that al, vuhyche prayth in the temple ma
be hard.

II. PARALIP. VI.

Salomon Roy Benit les aſſiſtans,
Rend grace à Dieu, des promeſſes parfaictes,
Priant pour ceux, qui ſeront perſiſtans
Es oraiſons, qu'agreables ſoyent faictes.

Sesac kyng of Egypt, by cause the Ieuuas
had forsaken the lord, takyth auuay the
shelds of gold, vuhyche Salomõ made, and
al the treasures of the houust of God.

II.   PARALIP.   XII.

Vn Roy d'Egypte, aux Iuifz tous vaincuz,
(Pourtant qu'auoyent laißé Dieu leur Seigneur)
Osta thresors, boucliers d'or, & escuz,
Que Salomon auoit faict pour honneur.

Sennacherib a blaſphemar inuadith the Ieuues, Ezechias exhortith the peple to triſt in
God. As Ezechias praed , the angel of God
ſeued the Aſſyrians.

II.   PARALIP.   XXXII.

Sennacherib en Iudée fait guerre,
Ezechias le peuple en Dieu exhorte,
Et luy priant, Aſſyriens par terre
L'ange pourſuit en ſa puiſſance forte.

Cyrus inſpired of God, dyd reſtore the veſ-
ſels of the temple, vuhych Nabuchodono-
ſor dyd tak auuay, he ſendith the peple aga
ne to buyld Ieruſalem.

I.   ESDRAE   I.

Le Roy Cyrus de Dieu bien inſpiré,
Rend les vaiſſeaux pour faire au temple office:
Puis il permit(comme eſtoit deſiré,)
Ieruſalem eſtre en ſon edifice.

Nehemias kyng Artaxerxis buttelar, prayth
vnto God for the resideuu of the peple of
Ierusalem, vuhyche vuar in truble.

II. ESDRAE I.

Nehemias seruant Artaxerxes,
(Pleurant à Dieu, pour la captiuité
De tous Iuifz) eut au Roy tel acces,
Qu'il luy permit refaire la Cité.

Iofias in the XIIII.mone of the fyrſt monetl in
Ierufalem offerith vp the paſchal lamb.

Iofias Roy treſſainƈt ſe remembra
Du temps paſſé:ɇ en Ierufalem
Sacrifiant,la Paſque celebra
Iour quatorzieſme,au premier mois de l'an.

Tobias is taken pryfoner of the Affyriãs. Vu
hen he dyd flepe by the vual ,the dung of
the fualouues did fal in his eyn vuherby he
vuas made blynd.

TOBIAE I. & II.

Le bon Tobie eftant captif & vieulx
Dormoit vn iour,& lors vne arondelle
Eftant là pres,fienta fur fes yeulx,
Dont perd la veue,& la clarté tant belle.

Satan obtanyth licence of God to deſtroye
al the goods of Iob and his chylder. Buth
he praſeth God in hys affliction.

Iob   I.

Iob par Satan(ayant de Dieu licence)
Souffre en ſes biens grand perſecution:
Ses enfans perd,dont il a patience,
Louant ſon Dieu en telle affliction.

Eliphaz rebukith Iob for the arrogancy of
vuyſdum and clenlynes. He deſcribith the
maledictiõ of the vuykked vuyche he doth
falſly attribute vnto Iob.

Iob XV.

A l'affligé donnant affliction
Eliphaz, Iob argue d'arrogance:
Et des mauuais la malediction
Mal attribue à ſa iuſte innocence.

The lord fpekyth vnto Iob, sheuuyng vnto
hym his rigtrtouſnes by his vnſerehable
vuorks. Vnto Iob is reſtored duple ryches
for that, that vuas taken from hym.

IOB.   XXXVIII. & XLII

Iob a de Dieu les propos entendus,
Luy demonſtrant par ſes œuures haultames
Sa grand' iuſtice, & au double rendus
Luy ſont ſes biens, & richeſſes mondaines.

K.

Aſſuerus makyng a gret feſt doth ſet ouut
his glori vaſthi his vuyſe diuorſed, Eſther
is made queyn.

Esther.   I. & II.

Aſſuerus celebrant vn conuiue
Repudia Vaſthi pour ſon orgueil,
Eſther trouua en ſa beauté ſi viue,
Qu'il la feit Royne auec vn grand recueil.

Vuhen Iudith had finifhed hir praet, she a-
nornyth hir vuyth garmenes of pleafur, to
the intent she shudl ouercome Holoforne ∙
for the glory of God.

IVDITH   X.

Iudith ayant faict oraifon latente,
Parée s'eft d'abitz de pompe, & gloire:
D'Holofernes puis s'en va vers la tente,
Pour à l'honneur de Dieu auoir victoire.

Iudith , vuhen Holofern vuas druncken and
ſlped, hir made kopyng the dore , ded cut
of his hede and caried it vnto hir citiſens.

IVDITH   XIII.

Holofernes yure comme vne beſte
S'endort, la fille eſt au guet à la porte:
A luy dormant Iudith trenche la teſte,
Qu'en Bethulie à ſes citoyens porte.

Dauid inſpiret vuith the ſpret of God , deſ-
cribyth the felicitits of man, he declared al
ſo the deſtruction of the vngadly and inſi-
deles.

PSALM.   I.

Dauid parlant par le Sainct eſperit,
Du bien heureux dict les beatitudes:
Et du mauuis recite qu'il perit,
Car en malice il a mis ſes eſtudes.

The pſalmiſt is angrye vuith the Ieuues and callith them fools vuhyche vngodly and vnfaytfully dēyeth Chriſt to be the treuue Meſſias and God, vuhyche yuas promyſed in the lauue.

PSALM. LII.

Folz ſont ceux là (comme eſcrit le Pſalmiſte)
Qui en leurs cueurs dient que Ieſus Chriſt
N'eſt Meſſias, Dauid tant ſ'en contriſte,
Qu'en pluſieurs lieux encontre iceux eſcrit.

Chrift fittyth ath the rigrhand of his father.
God the father gyuidh vnto his fon a prey
flly dignitye vuhyce shal luer in due for
the benefice of his paffion.

PSALM.   CIX.

Iefus Crift fiet de fon Pere à la dextre,
Qui pour loyer de fa mort trefcruelle
La dignité luy donne de grand prebftre,
Qui eft fans fin durante, & eternelle.

K 4

The incomprehensible mysteri of the loue
vuhiche Christ harbre touuard his spouus
the chyrce, and agane, that the chyrche
hath touuard Christ, is fully expressed.

CANTICOR. I.

Salomon Roy au liure des Cantiques
Propos d'amy vers vne amie expose,
L'amour couurant soubz parolles mystiques
De Christ enuers l'Eglise son espouse.

Iſaias doth lament the ſyns of Ieruſalem, the
lord doth reiect by Iſaias hys prophet the
ceremonies of the Ieuues, vuherin they did
put ther truſt.

ESAIAE.   L.

Plourant, lamente Iſaie prophete
Du peuple Iuiſ les grandz pechez, & vices:
Puis Dieu (par luy) de ce peuple reiette
L'hypocriſie auec leurs ſacrifices.

L

Eſaias doth ſe the glory of God and atkno-
legeth his ſins. By the token and the vuord
he obtanith remiſſion of ſins, and is ſent vnto the Ieuues.

ESAIAE. VI.

De Dieu la gloire Iſaie apperçoit,
De ſon peché il a la congnoiſſance:
L'ange le touche, & pardon il reçoit,
Tranſmis aux Iuifz par diuine puiſſance.

Ezechias is ded ſeyk. He receauitk a token of
helth of the lord in his natiuitye.

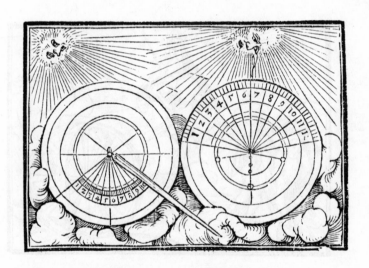

Ezechias iuſqu'à la mort malade,
En l'horoſcope eut ſigne de ſanté:
Contre ſon cours le ſoleil retrograde
De dix degreʒ, ou il eſtoit monté.

L 2

The visions of Ezechiel of the fouur bests, of the vuheyls, of the thron, and the image vuhich sittyth vpon the thron.

EZECH.   I.

Ezechiel voit en sa vision
Dieu en son throne, auec les quatre bestes:
L'aigle, le Beuf, & l'Homme, & le Lion,
Roues aussi de tourner tousiours prestes.

The reſtoryng of the citye and the temple
is ſheuued vnto Ezechiel the prophet in vi-
ſions.

EZECH.   XL.

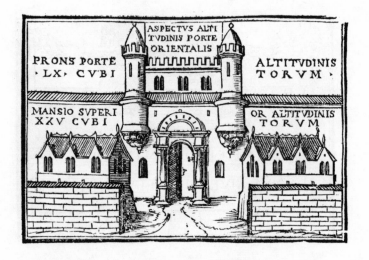

Monſtré luy eſt en contemplation
De ſon eſprit, qui le futur contemple
A l'aduenir, la reſtauration
De la Cité, & du ſouuerain Temple.

L 3

Ezechiel doth ſe the glory of God putre in
to the temple vuhiche it had forſaken: the
meſures of the altar ar deſcribed.

EZECH.   XLIII.

Puis voit apres du grand Dieu immortel
La haulte gloire en ce ſainct temple entrer:
Et la longueur, & largeur de l'autel,
Vient par meſure à deſcrire, & monſtrer.

Ezechiel feyth vuaters rinnyng ouut of the
temple, the cofts and diuifions of the laude
of promiffion, by the lord ar sheuued vnto
the prophet.

EZECH.   XLVII.

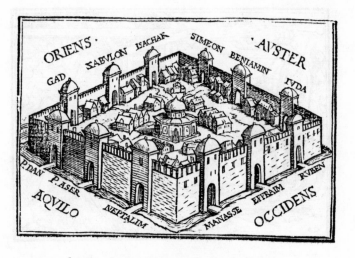

Ezechiel voit du temple eaux coulantes,
Et les confins de la promiffion,
Des douze auffi lignées excellentes,
Monftrée à luy eft la diuifion.

Sidrah, Misach, and Abdenago ar casten in to a fornce of fyre, by cause the vuold not vuorshyppe the gelden image contrary vn to the kyngs decrit.

DANIELIS IIII.

Au four ardant(car le Roy l'institue)
Sidrach, Misach, Abdenago sont mis,
Pource qu'ilz n'ont adoré sa statue,
Mais Dieu en fin deliure ses amis.

A viſion of fouur beſts is ſheuued vnto Daniel. Tis viſion is interpreted of four kyng-
doms of the vuorld.

Daniel voit les quatre ventz combatre,
De leurs eſpritz mauuais ſpirans leſpires,
Beſtes auſſi iuſqu'au nombre de quatre,
Signifians du monde quatre empires.
                    M

Daniel seyth the fygthyng letuuen a ram
and a gotbuke. The ynderstamdinh of the
vision is declared vnto Daniel bi the angel.

DANIELIS   VIII.

Il voit apres vne bataille forte,
Entre vn mouton, & vn bouc tout cornu:
L'ange parlant luy expose, & raporte
Ce que sera sur la fin aduenu.

The prophecy of Daniel of the kyngs of the
Perſians, of the kyngdom of Grece, of Egy
pte, and the treuues of it, and the battele vuyth the kyngdom of Syria is prophecyed.

DANIELIS   XI.

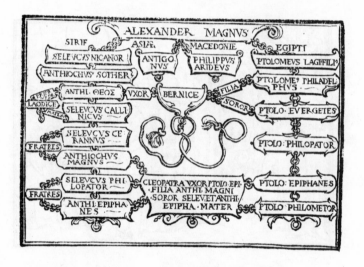

*Puis il predit des faictz des Roys de Perſe,
De Grece, Egypte, & des Roys de Syrie:
Prophetiſant mainte guerre diuerſe,
Pour agrandir chaſcune ſeigneurie.*

DANIELIS XIII.

Susanne fut accusée à grand tort
Par deux vieillardz, mais par raison decente
Daniel ieune enfant, iuge à la mort
Les accuseurs, l'accusée innocente.

Daniel for the diſtroyng of Bel and the Dra
gon is caſten in to the den of lions. Abacuc
doth bring meat.

Le grand dragon, auec l'idole Bel
Furent deſtruictz. Et pour ce faict fut mis
Dedans le lac aux lions Daniel:
Pour le nourrir Habacuc eſt tranſmis.

OSEAE I.

Osee prend, & espouse vne femme
Fornicatrice, & trois enfans eut d'elle:
Signifiant l'idolatrie infame
Du peuple Iuif, peu vers son Dieu fidelle.

Iohel prophicieth the diſtruction of Ieruſalem. He exortyth the preyſts vnto praer
and faſtyng for the calamitye vuhyche
vuas at hand.

IOELIS I.

Ioel predit de la deſtruction
Ieruſalem, & au prebſtres ſupplie,
Vacquer à iune, & à deuotion,
Et oraiſon d'humilté remplie.

M 4

Amos doth prophycit aganſt Damaſc , the
Philiſtians, Tyrus, Idumia , and teh ſons of
Ammon.

AMOS   I.

Contre Damas, Philiſthins, Idumée,
Et contre Tyr, auec les filz Ammon,
Sa prophetie Amos ſi l'a ſemée
En brief parler, & ſoubz obſcur ſermon.

Ionas is sent in to the rity of Niniuem for to preche , he his pumished by cause his pro-phycy vuas not fulfilled aganst Niniuem.

IONAE   I. II. III.

Affligé fut par tempeste soudaine
Ionas transmis en Niniue precher,
Trois iours au ventre il fut d'une Balaine,
Puis vers Niniue il se print à marcher.
                    N

Habacuc carying potage and brede vnto the repers in the perſon of holi men doth godly complane, that miſdoers doth perſecute the rightus.

Portant des pains Habacuc le prophete
Aux moiſſonneurs & laboureurs des champs,
Se plaint à Dieu de ce qu'iniure est faicte
Aux gens de bien, par les felons meſchantz.

Zachary doth monishe the peple that the
shuld conuert them self vnto God, and es-
keuu the luel doyngs of ther for fathers.

Zacharias tout le peuple admoneste
Se conuertir au Seigneur Dieu puissant,
Et euiter le peché deshonneste
De ses parentz, ou est chascun glissant.

Vuhen Antiochus did prepare his secōd pro
fection in to Egypt vuonder ful tokēs vuas
seyn in the aer at Ierusalem.

II.   MACHAB.   V.

Antiochus faisant aux Iuifz la guerre,
On veit au ciel dessus Ierusalem
Hommes armez, tout ainsi qu'en la terre,
Lors prinse fut pour les Iuifz en mal an.

L'autheur.

Qvand vous aurez contemplé ces Images
   Du Dieu viuant, ayes en souuenir
La grand puissance, & merueilleux ouurages,
Et sa bonté qui nous peut subuenir.
   Ce vous sera profit à l'aduenir
D'estudier telle philosophie:
Vueillez le sens de l'Eglise tenir,
La lettre occit, & l'esprit viuifie.

Plus que moins.

Matthæus Euangelista.

Marcus Euangelista.

Lucas Euangelista

Ioannes Euangelista.

MATVRA.

ACHEVÉ D'IMPRIMER
SUR LES PRESSES OFFSET DE L'IMPRIMERIE REDA S.A.
A CHÊNE-BOURG (GENÈVE), SUISSE

JUILLET 1973